BACKROADS
OF
AMERICA

BACKROADS
= OF =
AMERICA

by
Michael McKeever

Ideals Publishing Corporation
Nashville, Tennessee

Dedicated to Suzanne Berner
and her daughter
and her granddaughter

ISBN 0-8249-4036-9
Copyright © MCMLXXXIX by Ideals Publishing Corp.
Nelson Place at Elm Hill Pike
Nashville, TN 37214
All rights reserved.
Printed and bound in U.S.A.

Cover Photo
ORFORD, NEW HAMPSHIRE
Fred Sieb Photography

Photo Opposite
BLUE RIDGE PARKWAY AT ROCK KNOB
NORTH CAROLINA
Gene Ahrens/H. Armstrong Roberts, Inc.

CONTENTS

Photo Opposite
SOUTH PEACHAM, VERMONT
Fred Sieb Photography

HUTCHINS BRIDGE
MONTGOMERY CENTER, VERMONT
Gene Ahrens, Photographer

8

ROADS TO OUR PAST

JOHNNY APPLESEED

I n his long life, Jonathan Chapman never led soldiers to victory. He never ran for political office. He made no scientific discoveries, great or small. In matters of money he lived happily as a pauper.

Yet wherever he passed, he was welcome. He never wanted for food or shelter.

What Jonathan Chapman did was talk gently about good things like peace and love. And he planted trees—apple trees.

Throughout the Indiana frontier of the early 1800s, he was affectionately known as Johnny Appleseed.

Unlike Paul Bunyan or Pecos Bill, Johnny Appleseed was no myth. He was born in 1774. While in his mid-twenties, he felt the call to travel the new frontier, preaching his faith. And along the way, he softened the wilderness with apple trees.

He collected apple seeds from Pennsylvania's cider mill. Then he set out westward, walking alone, planting as he went. Traveling up the Ohio River Valley, he crossed into Indiana. When his leather pouches were emptied of seeds, he returned to Pennsylvania for more.

For forty-six years the cycle was repeated uncounted times. Before his work was done, Johnny Appleseed's orchards were scattered across 100,000 square miles. Many bear fruit to this day.

His wandering came to an end in 1845 in Allen County, Indiana. His final resting place in Fort Wayne is marked by a rugged stone engraved with a Bible and an apple.

Behind him he left us a wonderful legacy, renewed each spring when the wind brings the soft fragrance of apple blossoms.

THE PRINCIPLE OF THE THING

As burglaries go, it wasn't much. The stolen property in question was a small boat worth maybe thirty dollars. It had been pulled up on the sand next to the Little Missouri River.

During the night, thieves pushed it into the water and disappeared downstream. The wranglers at the Elkhorn Ranch said it wasn't worth going after. There are just too many places for someone on the run to hide in North Dakota's desolate Badlands.

And the weather had turned bitterly cold, with chunks of ice floating in the river. The sullen sky promised snow.

But the Elkhorn boss said it was the principle of the thing that mattered. So the grumbling cowboys hammered together a second boat. Then two of them and the boss set out in pursuit.

For two days the men pushed on, pelted by sleet and dodging ice. On the morning of the third day, they caught up with the thieves. With grim faces the men from the Elkhorn leveled their rifles. The thieves surrendered.

It took eight miserable days to return to civilization. Food ran out and the weather worsened. Some they met along the way suggested hanging the thieves from the nearest tree.

But the boss of the Elkhorn said no. He said lynching would violate the same principle that made him go after the thieves in the first place.

Later one of the cowboys, a man named Joe Ferris, was talking with a friend. "You know," Ferris remarked, "someday that man will be president of the United States."

Ferris was right. Theodore Roosevelt left the Elkhorn to return to politics. In 1901 he became the twenty-sixth president of the United States. And today the beach where he captured the thieves is part of the Theodore Roosevelt National Park.

Photo Opposite
LITTLE MISSOURI RIVER AND THE BADLANDS
THEODORE ROOSEVELT NATIONAL PARK
MEDORA, NORTH DAKOTA
Larry Burton, Photographer

CHILLS AND DELIGHTS FOR A QUARTER

Let us now mourn the loss of two-headed snakes and the petrified man and chickens who tapped out "Yes Sir, That's My Baby" on tiny pianos.

There's no question that the highway system is a noble achievement. These ribbons of concrete slashing across the landscape bind our nation together as they make travel both swift and efficient. They are a vast improvement over the two-lane highways that once wandered leisurely from city to city.

But future generations will miss the gawdy, tacky, wonderful roadside attractions that thrilled, chilled, and delighted us. And all for a quarter or so. Most have already vanished from our roadsides along with Burma Shave signs and free gas station maps.

The signs beckoned as we neared. "DRAGONS OF THE DESERT TEN MILES AHEAD!" Then "REAL LIVE DRAGONS FIVE MILES AHEAD!" And finally "SEE THEM IF YOU DARE! ONLY TWENTY-FIVE CENTS!"

Mother groaned but father settled the matter by pointing out that it was bound to be educational. And if the dragons turned out to be a couple of sleepy Gila monsters, well, we didn't really care. The soda pop was cold and it was nice to get out and walk around.

Happily there are still places where one can be filled with wonder for a few cents or even for free.

At the Fick Fossil and History Museum in Oakley, Kansas, one can still see the Great Seal of the United States crafted entirely of sharks' teeth. At the Tomahawk Trading Post in White's City, New Mexico, you can still pitch pennies into a wishing well filled with hissing rattlesnakes. And little boys still press wet noses against the glass to stare at "Sylvester Mummy" in Seattle's Ye Olde Curiosity Shop.

But alas! Such places are becoming fewer and fewer.

Photo Opposite
YE OLDE CURIOSITY SHOP
SEATTLE, WASHINGTON
Jeffrey High/Image Productions

TOUCH THE RAILS

Years ago on a winter evening in Nevada when snow dusted the sage, I stopped by the highway. A railroad track paralleled the road. Twin rails, polished by uncounted wheels, gleamed in the sunset. A pinprick of light danced on the horizon.

The pinprick grew and the rails began to sing. Moments later a train roared past in a blur of yellow. It was the Union Pacific's crack *City of Los Angeles.*

We named our trains once. Names like *California Zepher* and *Super Chief.*

We even named the locomotives. We named them for the heroes we admired and women we loved. And we gave them names for their dignity and power like *Golden Eagle* and *The General.*

We decorated them lovingly with little painted scenes on the headlights and flags that snapped in the wind. We painted the cabs candy apple red with little stars on the hubs of their drive wheels.

There isn't time for that anymore.

Still, wherever you are today, there is probably a railroad track nearby. Touch the rails. Those rails connect to other rails which in turn are connected to still more rails. Eventually the rails will carry your touch to the vast switching yards of Chicago and along the Florida coast and across the Texas plains.

There is magic in your touch.

Photo Opposite
MAGIC RAILS
Steve Myers/International Stock Photo

DEVIL OF THE NORTH CAROLINA COAST

Almost three hundred years ago, a devil haunted the coast of North Carolina. It was a devil in human form and it had a name: William Teach. But it is by his nickname that he is remembered: Blackbeard the Pirate.

In his dark ship, the *Queen Anne's Revenge*, he cut a bloody swath across the high seas. And when his hold was swollen with loot, he slipped through narrow Ocracoke Inlet into shallow Pamlico Sound. There, while the king's warships prowled the Carolina coast, Blackbeard planned his murderous forays.

Through the years the hidden waterways and islands of North Carolina harbored a viper's nest of pirates. But none was more hated and feared than the ferocious Blackbeard.

In 1718, the colonial government dispatched Royal Navy Captain Robert Maynard to bring in Blackbeard, dead or alive. Maynard planned carefully. First he selected two swift vessels able to navigate Pamlico's waters. Then he hand-picked an all-volunteer crew.

On a fog enshrouded morning, Maynard's ships closed in on the *Queen Anne's Revenge*. One of the naval vessels ground to a halt on a sand bar. But Maynard pressed on in the other.

The battle raged as the ships stood hull to hull and shot it out. Then Maynard grappled Blackbeard's ship and boarded. In the savage hand-to-hand combat that followed, Blackbeard the Pirate died fighting on his quarterdeck, roaring defiance to the end.

And his treasure? Most likely it's somewhere along the North Carolina coast. As Blackbeard once said, "Nobody but me and the devil knows where the treasure is."

And Blackbeard is dead, which leaves only the devil.

VIRGINIA CITY, THE LIVING GHOST TOWN

Virginia City, Nevada, tumbles down the brown flanks of Mt. Davidson in a waterfall of old buildings, vacant lots, and memories. The hills surrounding the town are honeycombed with mine shafts.

Once shining rivers of gold and silver poured from the mines as Virginia City rivaled San Francisco as Queen of the West. Wealthy mine owners built mansions decorated with French wallpaper, English crystal chandeliers, and doorknobs of Nevada silver.

The town boasted four banks, an opera house, and 110 saloons, all of which did a rip-roaring business. People came from miles around just for the fun of riding in the only elevator between Chicago and San Francisco. Over a billion dollars in precious metals yielded to the dynamite and pick axes of the miners. But eventually the last of the high-grade ore was gouged from the earth. The merchants and miners, fancy ladies and gamblers moved on to the next strike.

However, unlike most western boom towns, Virginia City refused to die. Today, in no way a ghost town, it mines its past to please a growing tourist industry.

A century's worth of fires, harsh weather, and neglect have destroyed much of Virginia City. But enough has survived to evoke an era when glory holes dotted the hills and a miner could be a pauper one day and fabulously wealthy the next.

Audiences cheer the hero and hiss the villain in melodrama at Piper's Opera House. Visitors and locals alike wash down the Nevada dust in saloons with names like Silver Dollar and the Red Garter. And the *Territorial Enterprise* went to press every week up until a few years ago.

It was the editors of the *Enterprise* who hired a promising cub reporter to write humorous features under the byline "Josh." As his writing improved, he took on another pseudonym: Mark Twain.

ALCATRAZ ISLAND

It would seem an unlikely tourist attraction, this barren island in the middle of San Fancisco Bay. Yet so many come that reservations are required.

As the boat pushes off from the waterfront, its passengers are in a cheerful mood. Many are on vacation, and this afternoon will be a highlight of their visit to the fabled City by the Bay.

But as the boat nears its destination, the passengers become quiet. Ahead waits Alcatraz Island, the infamous "Rock." Here the worst criminals were sent, including those too tough for other prisons. Al Capone, Machine Gun Kelly, and "Bird Man" Robert Stroud did hard time here.

The last inmates, shackled in leg irons and waist chains, shuffled onto a prison boat in 1963. Ten years later Alcatraz opened to the public under the National Park Service.

Visitors step onto the island next to the naked steel guard tower that greeted arriving prisoners. A ranger, uniform sharply creased, makes a brief welcoming speech. The tour begins, following the same route that new convicts took into the bowels of the prison.

The group crosses "Times Square" in front of the dining hall and enters the bleak exercise yard. Once a week the prisoners were let out into the pale sunshine for two hours.

Eventually the tour steps onto "Broadway," the broad passage separating the two main cell blocks. Huddled against the chill, visitors peer between the bars into empty cells. The ranger's voice echoes in the huge building .

After a while the boat returns the tour to San Francisco. Fog rolls in from the Pacific, the rust-red towers of the Golden Gate Bridge rising above the billows. Fog horns begin their chorus.

For most of us, San Francisco's fog horns are a friendly, reassuring sound. But for the men on Alcatraz, they were a dirge.

Photo Opposite
ALCATRAZ BUILDINGS THROUGH
SALLYPORT WINDOW
GOLDEN GATE NATIONAL RECREATION AREA
SAN FRANCISCO BAY, CALIFORNIA
Jeff Gnass Photography

THE OLD FAMILIAR CIRCUS

Nowadays when the circus comes to town, it more than likely appears in an indoor arena. The big tops are rare now. Arenas are air-conditioned in the summer, heated in the winter, and spanking clean throughout.

This means the smell of the circus is missing: that wonderful blend of sawdust and strange animals and canvas hot in the sun. And with the smell have vanished circus sounds: barkers with raspy voices, laughter from clown alley, and the roar of the big cats.

Remember circus parades? The ringmaster, resplendent in scarlet coat and shiny black top hat, leading the way. Then eight white horses with yellow plumes, pulling the great steam calliope. And the elephants making their ponderous way down Main Street ridden by pretty ladies in sequined capes.

The people of Baraboo, Wisconsin, understand the wonder of such things. But then Baraboo's circus pedigree is long and honorable. Once five local boys started a backyard circus with some rabbits, a billy goat, and an elderly horse named Zachary which they bought for $8.42.

Their Baraboo neighbors knew them as "those Ringling kids." We know them as the Ringling Brothers and Barnum & Bailey Combined Circus, The Greatest Show on Earth.

Their old winter quarters in Baraboo now house the Circus World Museum. There are brightly colored railroad cars and a steam calliope that whistles and tootles. Twice a day in season, there are performances. Great gilded band wagons lumber by and colorful pennants snap in the breeze.

And there is this familiar smell, a wonderful blend of sawdust and strange animals and canvas hot in the sun.

No One Forgets His First Car

Like many American males, I'm sometimes a bit shaky on remembering important things like wedding anniversaries. But no one forgets his first car.

Mine was a Henry J, a pert little thing with a pug nose and saucy upturned rear fenders. True, she wasn't a long and lean aristocrat like the Packard. And she wasn't solid like the Hudson with its comfortable old easy chair of a rear seat that swallowed you up in its plush embrace.

But she was mine. And together we puttered down many a country road, all sixty-eight horses of the tiny engine happily galloping along.

Listen to the names of the great American cars, how they roll off the tongue with an easy grace: Pontiac and Pierce-Arrow, elegant Duesenberg and the Cord, a cherry red Stutz Bearcat with black leather seats that creaked when you sat down, Marmon and Auburn and the Tucker Torpedo.

Back in the days when automobiles had running boards, they also had hood ornaments. Remember Cadillac's art deco lady? Pontiac's Indian chief leaning into the wind? Lincoln's leaping greyhound? Even the no-nonsense Ford once sported a quail in flight.

No one knows what makes a classic, but the designers keep trying. Sometimes they fall right on their bumpers. I for one do not lament the late DeLorean. With its gull-wing doors extended, it looked like an albatross that crashed into a piling.

On the other hand, who can forget the '49 Studebaker with its curved rear window? Now that was a car.

Photo Opposite
1930 PACKARD
SUN VALLEY, IDAHO
Jack Williams, Photographer

HOBO CONVENTION

Greasy Frank probably won't make it. Steampot Willie says he'll try even though he's getting on in years. But White Plains Bill says he wouldn't miss it. He'll hop the Salad Bowl Express out of California, then catch a hotshot freight to Mason City.

From Mason City, Iowa, it's only eighteen miles to Britt. And Britt, as any self-respecting knight of the road knows, is home to the annual Hobo Convention.

Like the swallows who come back to Capistrano, hoboes have made their way back to Britt every August since 1896. There'll be a hobo parade and pots of simmering mulligan stew. A new hobo king and queen will be elected based on a two-minute speech from each of the candidates.

In the early years of this century, it wasn't unusual for a hundred or more hoboes to gather at Britt. For those men (and a few women) born to wander, the convention was a time to meet old friends and swap tall tales.

It still is. But with each passing year, the hoboes become fewer and older. They still come to Britt, but now it seems that around the campfires it's harder to remember the words to the old hobo songs.

When Jeff Davis was elected king of the hoboes at the 1913 convention, he said proudly that hoboes were ". . . men of good character, not yeggs, crooks, or bums."

There was a time when to be a hobo was to be a member of an honorable brotherhood. The ranks have grown thinner. But this year they will again gather at Britt, Iowa. They'll eat good stew and tell good stories and remember old friends. And there won't be a yegg or a crook or a bum among them.

Photo Opposite
LUPINE DECORATING
H. Armstrong Roberts, Inc.

DINOSAUR NATIONAL MONUMENT

Once there were giants in the land. As they strode through steaming tropical forests, the Utah earth shook under every step. It was the age of dinosaurs when misty swamps and vast seas covered the land.

The roar of the thunder lizards was silenced tens of millions of years ago. Yet they have not completely vanished from the earth.

True, the last dinosaur disappeared long before the first humans huddled together around a fire. But the earth, as if reluctant to forget the great beasts, has imprisoned their bones in stone.

Today almost every major natural history museum boasts at least one dinosaur skeleton.

Usually the most popular is the *Tyrannosaurus rex*. Even reduced to reconstructed and wired-together fossils, it is a terrifying creature.

Dinosaur National Monument is located amid the sandstone hills on the northern Utah-Colorado border. There, paleontologists patiently free the bones from their stone prison. Visitors are welcome to watch.

It is painstaking work, sometimes done with dental picks. As the fossils are released from the rock, they are brought to a nearby laboratory where scientists try to bring order to jumbles of often mismatched finds.

Most visitors come away from the monument filled with a sense of awe. At a museum, the fossils have been sorted and tagged and mounted. But at Dinosaur National Monument, you are as close to the dinosaurs as you will ever get.

When you look at the sheer rock, you are looking at ancient earth where huge creatures beyond our imagination stalked each other. And where their bones lay undisturbed since they died and fell into the primeval mud 140 million years ago.

BASKETMAKERS
COLONIAL WILLIAMSBURG, VIRGINIA
W. Metzen/H. Armstrong Roberts, Inc.

32

ROADS TO CRAFTS

SPLIT-RAIL FENCES

The names of the fence builders are mostly forgotten now, unfortunately. To be a rail splitter was no small thing.

It took a special sense of the wood, the ability to move your hands across the rough bark and know which way the grain ran and just where to put in the wooden wedges.

It took a keen eye to judge precisely where each rail should fit so that as the seasons turned, the fresh wood "married" into a solid fence.

And it took strength, not brutal strength but graceful strength to swing the hammer in long rhythmic arcs over and over.

In 1865 Abraham Lincoln journeyed to a Virginia battlefield for a counsel of war with his generals. Near headquarters, he passed a pile of firewood. Impulsively he seized the axe and for several minutes the blade bit into the wood. Then, raising the axe, Lincoln held it straight out and steady at the end of his arm. Weary though he was, the rail-splitter muscles of his youth did not fail him.

Today wood is cut and sliced and shaped amid the high-pitched whine of powerful saws. It is both efficient and anonymous. And in that is the rail splitters' triumph.

For though nameless, they have found immortality in their workmanship. Each time a traveler stops to admire the skill and care put into a split-rail fence, the craftsman who built it is remembered.

And that is a fine epitaph.

Photo Opposite
WOODLAND DAFFODILS
Milton Baroody/ Cyr Color Photo

Mountain Music

The hill people of Kentucky's southern Appalachians know what is true and good: blackberries plucked with the morning dew still on them and eaten in a bowl of rich cream; the smell of freshly turned earth under a plow; the pure, sweet music that has never strayed from its roots.

In small mountain communities and down in the winding hollows are the small white-boarded churches. Step inside on Sunday morning and listen. There are solemn hymns for solemn occasions. But in Appalachia, Sunday mornings are, as the bible says, time to "make a joyful noise unto the Lord."

Perhaps if you are very lucky, you'll hear music of the *Sacred Harp*, a collection of hymns virtually unchanged from their seventeenth-century English and Scottish lay roots. Mountain people sang music like this when Daniel Boone hunted game in these woods two hundred years ago.

Many of the area's earliest settlers came from the British Isles westward through the Cumberland Gap. Their music weaves through Appalachia like a memory recounting long-ago wars and lost loves.

In the evening people sit on front porches and pick at banjos and strum guitars and sing softly to themselves. Sometimes you'll hear the soothing, haunting sound of a three-string mountain dulcimer plucked with a feather.

Life in Appalachia can be hard. So when happy occasions arrive, like weddings and babies and homecomings, they are celebrated joyfully. Mandolins and fiddles are played into the night and tables are heavy with apple pies and cast-iron pots filled with baked beans.

After a while the fiddle player will take a break and the dancers will rest their feet. Someone will reach for a guitar, and soon the gentle, simple sounds of "Amazing Grace" and "Barbara Allen" will carry down the hollow, sweet and pure as a mountain stream.

Photo Opposite
DULCIMERS
Mack & Betty Kelly, Photographers

BALLOONS IN THE DESERT SKY

From an airplane the desert outside Albuquerque looked as if it had been covered by a gigantic crazy quilt. In the cold New Mexico morning, dozens of people were neatly spreading out brightly colored fabric.

Burners fueled by propane tanks roared into life and pumped hot air into the fabric. Slowly each patch of fabric lifted itself from the desert floor and became an inflated balloon. What had been a quilt was now a field of gaudy beach balls.

One by one the balloons lifted off and soared into the clear sky. Some left the ground with a lurch, others as softly as a baby's kiss. Suspended beneath each was a gondola.

Modern hot air balloons do not dance carefree on the wind; they must be skillfully piloted. The balloon's speed and altitude are carefully monitored, and great care is taken that the balloon does not "kiss," or bump into, another balloon.

For a few moments the balloon floats as lightly and silently as a cloud. Then there is a slight hiss of gas and the burner roars to life. Flames shoot upward, heating the air inside the balloon's "envelope." Periodically the pilot adjusts the blast valve controlling the burner.

All around, other balloons float in the still morning. The field of gaudy beach balls has become glistening soap bubbles set adrift in a robin's egg blue sky.

Eventually, in ones and twos, like children's circus balloons whose helium has tired, the balloons sink downward. Some land with a thump and a puff of dust, others as gently as leaves plucked by an autumn wind.

With each touchdown, laughter spills across the desert as champagne is uncorked in the traditional balloonists' toast to good friends and a successful flight.

Made with Much Love

Recently I made my little daughter a doll. I fashioned it out of clay and, as dolls go, it isn't anywhere nearly as polished as the toy-shop variety. But Penny loves it largely because Daddy made it, I suspect.

Which brings me to cornhusk, corncob, and applehead dolls. Nowadays, you find them in craft shows and the like. But there was a time when such dolls were made for young children by loving hands.

There were no shopping malls then. In the small towns and isolated farms of rural America, toys were the result of a parent's ingenuity.

Which made them all the more special.

When the first settlers arrived on the raw frontier, they found Indian children playing with cornhusk dolls. And more than one lonely settler's child soon had a similar doll with braided cornsilk hair as a playmate.

To play house properly, the girl doll in her cornhusk dress needed a boy doll. A corncob served as the body with an attached circle of cob as the head. With a bean nose and eyes drawn in with the stub of a pencil, a fit companion for the prettiest cornhusk maiden could be made.

Applehead dolls were often born on warm summer nights on the front porch. With a jackknife pulled from a pocket of a worn pair of overalls, rough features were carved on a fresh apple. As the apple dried, the face of a little old person appeared, ready to hear a child's secrets.

They couldn't walk, talk, or drink from a baby bottle. But they required no batteries. And like Penny's clay doll, they were made with much love.

QUILTS, OUR PATCHWORK HISTORY

I n old quilts, stitch by patient stitch, is the record of who we were, what we did, what pleased us, what saddened us.

Many, covered with swirling designs and exhuberant sunbursts, were created for the simple pleasure of making something beautiful. Others, made by desperately lonely women in prairie huts or New England seamen's wives watching the horizon, kept the mind from wandering. And still others were intended as political statements by abolitionists and suffragettes.

Some were created just for the fun of it. An 1880 quilt in the Denver Art Museum is decorated with silk cigar bands. A 1916 Massachusetts farm family passed a dreary winter creating a delightful quilt of characters from the funny pages. Other quilts, patched together from old baby blankets and uniforms and bits of silk from long-ago weddings, record a family's history.

And still others record the nation's history. In 1863 a lady named Adeline Sears stitched the signatures of 360 notable people into a quilt. Among those who answered her request for an autograph was Abraham Lincoln.

There are drums of distant wars in our quilts. One Union wife carefully listed all fifty-seven battles her husband fought in. There is a Southern quilt made of faded gray and butternut brown scraps of Confederate uniforms.

Not all quilts were stitched by women's hands. In the Shelburne, Vermont, Museum is a beautiful work created by a wounded Union soldier in the hospital. In the childhood homes of Dwight Eisenhower and Calvin Coolidge are quilts pieced together by the boyish hands of two future presidents.

Nor is quilting a lost art. In 1975 the New York City Museum of American Folk Art and the U.S. Historical Society sponsored a quilt contest. They were promptly buried under an avalanche of 10,000 entries.

Photo Opposite
COMFORTABLE QUILTS

THE AMERICAN LONG RIFLE

The making of an American long rifle began with fire. At a blacksmith's forge, a flat iron bar was held in the flames until it glowed red. Then, amid dancing sparks, it was hammered around a central core.

Slowly the bar was shaped into a rifle barrel. The barrel cooled. Then a hand-cranked reamer cleaned out the heart. The interior was grooved with spiral lines which caused the lead ball to spin, giving the rifle its legendary accuracy.

Meanwhile a stock of sturdy maple was carved to receive the barrel. Before the rifle would be finished, at least 300 hours of highly skilled craftsmanship was required.

To cast the fittings, a strong wooden box was filled with moist, fine-grained sand. Fittings from another rifle were pressed into the sand and then carefully removed. Brass was heated over flames into a boiling liquid. Then, very slowly to prevent bubbles, it was poured into the impression left in the sand.

After the rifle was assembled, it was taken out to be test-fired and sighted. If the workmanship was good, the lead ball left the barrel at around 2,000 feet per second. And after the master gunsmith had sighted the rifle, it would be accurate enough to easily bring down wild game at a hundred or more yards.

Finally the rifle was polished and filed and engraved. On the frontier the crack of the long rifle fed the settler's family and protected their home. And at Lexington and Concord, it was midwife to the birth of a new nation.

CARRIAGES: IT'S ALL IN THE WHEELS

True carriage connoisseurs can tell an American carriage from its European cousins at a glance. Not that foreign vehicles didn't have a beauty all their own.

British carriages, like the Victoria with its graceful curves and lofty coachman's seat, fairly reeked of elegance. Enough so that gilded age tycoons of the late nineteenth century imported them as rolling status symbols like today's luxury cars.

But for all the British carriage's dignity, the wooden spokes on its wheels were thick, heavy things of solid English oak. The American spokes, on the other hand, were long and slim and weighed much less.

The secret was in the hickory wood from which the American spokes were fashioned. In all their vast empire, the British could not boast of any wood as light yet as strong as hickory.

Good carriages did not come cheap. A basic runabout could be ordered from a catalog for around $35. But a really first-rate carriage could go for a hundred dollars or more. And this was a time when $3.50 for ten hours was rated a good day's pay.

Of course the carriage was entirely hand-crafted and covered by over twenty alternating coats of paint and varnish. Options were available at a price. Seats, for example, were usually upholstered with heavy cloth. But if price was no object, fine leather upholstery could be arranged for an additional $1.50.

With the coming of the automobile, many carriages were banished to the back of the barn or simply abondoned in vacant lots. The body weathered away and field mice took up residence in the upholstery. Eventually nothing was left except steel springs and the wheels with their long, slim hickory spokes.

WHAT A DUCK OUGHT TO LOOK LIKE

I n 1918 Lem and Steven Ward hung up the clippers and locked up their barbershop. The Ward brothers were Chesapeake Bay born and bred. And like anyone else with Chesapeake water in their veins, they knew what a duck ought to look like. So they started carving.

In place of the barber pole went a sign reading "L.T. Ward & Brother, Wildfowl Counterfeiters in Wood." In other words: decoys.

Duck decoys have been around almost as long as hunters. In dry western caves, fragile little birds of twigs and mud have been found amid the broken Indian pottery.

But what made the Ward decoys different was their astonishingly realistic appearance. A Ward decoy bobbing on the water was so lifelike, it was in danger of being shot. And they were so lovely, it seemed a shame to put them out in the water.

Soon other carvers along the eastern seashore from New York down to the Carolinas were creating their own beautiful works. The humble decoy had become an American art form.

Modern hunters' decoys are mass-produced in tough, durable plastic. But there are still artists who painstakingly carve their decoys, smoothing the wood and delicately painting the sheen of wet feathers. Some create little set pieces, with blades of carved grass and graceful metal cattails.

But no matter how elaborate the creation, at its heart is a wooden duck carved by someone who, like Lem and Steve Ward, knows what a duck ought to look like.

Photo Opposite
WOOD DUCK
H. Armstrong Roberts, Inc.

DANCING HORSES AND CHEERFUL BEARS

T here are those of us to whom Daniel Carl Muller and Salvatore Carnigliaro are Old Masters worthy of the same respect accorded Michelangelo and Raphael. And when one of their works is lost, we mourn because they are irreplaceable.

What Muller and Carnigliaro created were carousel animals. They and other master carvers like Arthur Anderson and C.J. Spooner and John Zalar created a wondrous world of fantastic creatures prancing in endless circles. Most worked around the turn of the century. Behind them they left a whimsical legacy of dancing unicorns and roaring lions and frogs dressed in elegant waistcoats.

Once 4,000 wooden merry-go-rounds spun their magic all over the United States. Today less than 200 carry on. Of these, only around eighty still boast the old hand-carved animals of the masters. The rest have had to fall back on modern mass-produced fiberglass horses of little detail and less imagination.

There were several carousel factories, each with its own artists and style. The Philadelphia Toboggan Company favored patriotic subjects like horses pulling chariots garnished with golden eagles, fluttering American flags, and Miss Liberty wielding the Sword of Justice. Loof was known for horses with flowing manes and saddles dripping with gilt trappings. Herschell-Spillman was noted for its folksy, friendly animals: giant dogs, cheerful bears, and strutting chickens.

Today many of the great carousels that enchanted earlier generations have been lost. But here and there across the country, others have been preserved to spin their magic for generations yet to come.

SAWTOOTH MOUNTAINS AND
LOWER REDFISH LAKE, IDAHO
Tom Algire Photography

52

ROADS OF WATER

STEAMBOAT ROUND THE BEND

Among my treasures I count two small, yellowing slips of paper. The first is a ticket good for one passage on a steamboat of the Memphis and St. Louis Packet Company.

I have my choice of boats; there are several listed on the back. They have splendid names like *Belle of St. Louis* and *City of Cairo* and the *Mary E. Forsyth*.

I don't know what they looked like, but I have a good idea. On the front of the ticket is an engraved illustration of a sidewheeler and it looks grand indeed. Smoke is rolling from tall twin stacks and her paddles are whipping the Mississippi to a lacy froth. She looks as imposing as a wedding cake, as graceful as a white swan.

The second bit of paper is the morning menu for the steamboat *W. R. Arthur*. Her captain was Patrick Yore and he took pride in the table he set for his passengers.

For breakfast there was beafsteak and mutton and pork chops, kidney pie and veal cutlets and jambalaya. There were muffins and cornbread, piping hot from the oven. There was coffee and tea, of course, and "breakfast wines to be had at the bar."

A century and more has passed since the last breakfast call on the *W. R. Arthur*; and I'm afraid my ticket from the Memphis and St. Louis Packet Company will do me no good. Her proud boats long ago vanished from the river.

Today a few steamboats still cruise the rivers, mostly carrying tourists bound for no place in particular. The merchants and gamblers and roustabouts are no more. And with them have gone glistening chandeliers and crisply monogrammed linens and gilt eagles perched atop pilot houses.

But in these two slips of paper, a sliver of time is frozen like the petals of a long-ago flower caught in amber.

In my imagination the *Belle of St. Louis* is just rounding the bend, her bow white with cotton bales and a plume of smoke rolling from her stacks. Should she stop at my landing, I have my ticket.

Photo Opposite
DELTA QUEEN STEAMBOAT
DELTA & MISSISSIPPI QUEEN STEAMBOAT CO.
NEW ORLEANS, LOUISIANA
Graphic Communications

55

MORNING ON THE SCHUYLKILL RIVER

The Schuylkill River gleams in the early morning light with the pale luminescence of a pearl. Around it, the city of Philadelphia yawns and stretches and awakens to a new day. But on the river, the rowers in their racing shells and single sculls pull to their own rhythm.

Theirs is one of the most solitary of sports. Sometimes with others but often alone, they propel their fragile crafts, hulls as slim as Shaker chairs, across the water's mirror surface. The only sounds are the measured breathing of the rowers and the faint splash of oars slicing the river.

In the 1870s Thomas Eakins painted a series of elegantly precise studies of rowers on the Schuylkill. Eakins enjoyed rowing and often his paintings evoke the purity of the lone athlete seeking to please only himself.

In his painting of his friend Max Schmitt near the Girard Avenue Bridge, Schmitt pauses alone in his scull. His image reflected in the water, he stares out of the painting at us as if we are intruders.

Not all of Eakins' Schuylkill paintings are of lone athletes. Sometimes, in the background, people line the banks at Fairmount Park, watching the race. But the rowers in the foreground face away from the crowd.

A hundred years and more have passed since Eakins. In the cold morning, rowers pull their oars in graceful sweeps leaving a series of tiny rippled circles behind them. Along the Schuylkill's banks, the roads fill with commuters flowing into downtown Philadelphia.

The rowers turn their crafts toward boathouses where they will be lifted dripping from the water. Then, still alone with their thoughts, they disappear into the city.

IN PRAISE OF SMALL FERRIES

They were huge, the ferries of my Pacific Northwest youth, small ships really, pushing their bows into the chilly gray waters of Puget Sound. Squadrons of sea gulls wheeled overhead as they passed rocky shorelines edged with dark forests.

They had Indian names that smelled of smoked salmon and carried the sound of potlatch drums in their heavy consonants. Names handed down from the people of the raven, of the bear, of the killer whale. Mighty names for mighty ferries.

In my boyhood I thrilled to the throb of powerful engines far below the deck and propellers that chopped the water into lacy froth. But in my maturity I have learned to value serenity as well. So it is that I have come to love small ferry boats.

Recently I began the day with a ferry trip across the James River in Virginia. By James River standards, I suppose the ferry would be middle-sized: larger than the explorers' ships that first sailed up her broad mouth yet smaller than General Grant's gunboats.

It was early; the morning mists still lay softly on the riverbank pines. At nearby Jamestown, a full-sized replica of an Elizabethan galleon pulled half-heartedly at her moorings; her flag limp in the still air.

The small ferry pulled away from the slip. In her wake the reeds along the shoreline danced.

Photo Opposite
MISSISSIPPI RIVER CAR FERRY
NORTH BUENA VISTA, IOWA
B. Vogel/H. Armstrong Roberts, Inc.

THE SALMON RIVER

From middle summer into fall, the Salmon River of Idaho is, while hardly placid, at least well mannered. But when spring comes to the Sawtooth Range, the melting snow makes its way down to the river and the swollen Salmon runs fast and dangerous.

The normally clear water becomes milky with silt. Driftwood, torn from the banks, is flung downstream by the current. Beaver dams are brushed aside. For weeks the Salmon is an unruly bully of a river.

Finally, about when July gives way to August, the snowpack is spent. The Salmon calms down. The water is still swift and cold as it swirls around boulders and surges over gravel bars. But the silt has settled, and steelhead trout can be seen flashing just beneath the surface.

The river is at its most beautiful. At little towns along its banks, canoes, kayaks, and rubber rafts are put into the water. From all over the west, people have come to run the Salmon.

At the same time, wranglers lead packtrains of visitors into the Sawtooth and White Cloud high country. During the day, they cross sunlit meadows bright with wildflowers. At night they sleep to the soft murmur of wind blowing through the trees.

With fall the chill wind ripples the lakes and there is a strange urgency in the air. In the Salmon River, forty-pound Chinook salmon end their 900-mile voyage home from the sea. At the Sawtooth Fish Hatchery, the miracle begins anew as they lay their eggs.

Winter is announced by snow flurries dancing in the mountain passes. The sky turns sullen, and soon the Salmon is smothered in white.

Photo Opposite
SALMON RIVER AND SAWTOOTH MOUNTAINS
IDAHO
George and Monserrate Schwartz, Photographers

BARELY A RIPPLE; THE CANAL BOATS

In the early nineteenth century, there was no more sedate or genteel a way to travel than by canal boat. Pulled at a plodding four miles an hour by patient mules, the long boats slipped along the canals with barely a ripple.

Stagecoaches were faster, but roads were rough and dangerous. Steamboats were more luxurious, but the slim canal boats moved up tight waterways forbidden to the aristocratic steamboats.

Ladies and gentlemen sat warming themselves in the sun on the upper deck, careful to mind the low bridges. The casual pace of the boat allowed one to enjoy the passing scenery. Here and there the canal narrowed and gentlemen plucked wildflowers from the bank for their ladies.

Fares were based on distance, usually about a nickel a mile. Meals were hardy and filling. Sometimes they were prepared in a tiny galley; other times taken on board from a canal-side inn.

Accommodations aboard the elegant little boats were cramped. When Charles Dickens traveled by canal, he mistook the bunks on his boat for bookshelves.

Eventually the canal boats, like the stagecoaches and steamboats, were done in by railroads. Early trains, belching smoke and sparks, could rattle down the track at a breathtaking fifteen miles an hour.

Today few canals remain. Joggers pad down the tow paths and the only canal boats are museum models.

That is, unless you happen to be driving down Ohio Route 93, southeast of Columbus. At Canal Fulton Park, a section of the Ohio-Erie Canal has been preserved. Several afternoons a week, a patient mule is hitched up to a boat. And with barely a ripple, you can take a two-mile trip into our unhurried and genteel past.

THE EAGLES OF CHILKAT

When the Alaskan winter comes to the Chilkat River, the wind whips through the dense forest like an icy knife blade. Snow falls from leaden skies and rivers and streams freeze into hard, white marble slabs.

But even in December, the warmer Chilkat flows freely, and her waters are filled with salmon who have fought their way home from the sea to spawn. It is also the time the bald eagles gather along her banks, the cottonwoods bending under their weight.

Forced out of their coastal nesting areas by ice and snow, the eagles come to feed on the salmon. By the end of the season, as many as 3,000 will gather along the Chilkat.

The bald eagle is both a majestic and fearsome creature. As it soars on wings reaching up to seven feet from tip to tip, its pale eyes miss little. While content to feast on carrion, its favorite prey is fish. Dropping from the sky like a thunderbolt, the eagle snatches salmon from the water with needle-sharp talons.

In most of the United States, the bald eagle survives in an uneasy compromise with our growing population. But in the Alaskan vastness, there is still room to be wild and free. And when winter comes to the Chilkat, the eagles will return as they always have.

Photo Opposite
BALD EAGLES AT CHILKAT RIVER
ALASKA
Kurt Ramseyer, Photographer

CAPITOL REEF
NATIONAL PARK, UTAH
Gene Ahrens, Photographer

ROADS TO OUR HERITAGE

TROOPER MIKE

Trooper Mike was recently laid to rest in the brown Montana earth. A squad from his regiment, the Seventh Cavalry, fired a salute. A bugler sounded taps and the soft notes carried down into the valley of the Little Big Horn.

We don't know much about Trooper Mike, not even his real name. His skeleton told the scientists that he was young, as most soldiers are, and that he fought hard and to the end. We know this because of the marks left by the bullets on his ribs and the place where he was hit by a warclub.

We know this happened in 1876 on a warm June afternoon when dragonflies danced above the Little Big Horn River. It was the time the Sioux called the Moon of Making Fat. The village stretched along the river, the air thick with the haze of uncounted campfires. The grass was cropped short by thousands of war ponies. George Armstrong Custer charged and the Seventh Cavalry followed.

An Indian later said that the Sioux and Cheyenne were as "many as the leaves on the trees." The warriors, he said, swarmed across the river "like bees from a hive."

Trooper Mike lay in the tall grass for over a century with only the wind for company. When he was finally found, his bones were lifted gently from the soil and cleaned. One foot still wore a cavalry boot.

A Cheyenne medicine man offered a prayer for peace. Then the lost trooper was laid to rest among his comrades on the hillside, alone no longer.

Photo Opposite
CUSTER BATTLEFIELD NATIONAL MONUMENT
CROW AGENCY, MONTANA
Larry Burton, Photographer

Maybe it's the stubborn streak of independence that runs through the state's history. New Hampshire, with the sturdy motto Live Free or Die, was the first colony to write its own constitution. It is the granite state, the land of Daniel Webster.

Maybe it's just the beauty of the place, from rock-walled farmers' fields to the white clapboard villages with their steepled churches and grassy commons. And whose soul could not be nourished by the glory of a New England fall?

Whatever the reason, artists and writers and musicians have long found their inspiration in the uplands and valleys of New Hampshire. This small, quiet northeast corner of America has enriched us all with the creativity of her sons and daughters. Some were born in her towns and tranquil countryside; others came and were made welcome.

There are the poets. John Greenleaf Whittier lived full of honors and years at Hampton Falls. Robert Frost once said that nearly half of his poems were written in New Hampshire. And the gentle Joyce Kilmer wrote "Trees" after strolling through the woods near Swanzy.

And there are the artists. José Orozco came from Mexico to teach and paint his defiant murals at Dartmouth. Maxfield Parrish came to Plainfield to paint his ethereal creations. Augustus Saint-Gaudens sculpted in his studio at Aspet.

Then there are the writers. Thornton Wilder looked at New Hampshire's villages and saw *Our Town*. Others, like Willa Cather and Stephen Vincent Benet, came to be nurtured at the MacDowell Artists' Colony at Peterborough.

Aaron Copland came to Peterborough and heard the wind rustling through fall foliage and creeks trickling across meadows. In his music he shares them with us.

Photo Opposite
AUTUMN
Universal Media, Inc.

COURAGE AT CAPE CANAVERAL

The Kennedy Space Center is on the Florida coast where Cape Canaveral nudges into the Atlantic. To enter, drive out the NASA Parkway past the Indian River where alligators laze along the banks and herons fly across the marshes. Soon you'll arrive at "Spaceport U.S.A." with its Visitors' Center and rows of parked cars glistening in the Florida sun.

The shells of several rockets stand ouside the center on display. One, a massive Saturn 1B, lies on its side like a toppled dinosaur, its white paint the color of bleached bones.

When the rockets fly, the ground trembles as they lift off and the sky glows with the fire of their engines. Yet, for all their majesty, the rockets are vulnerable. The star voyagers of the Challenger were doomed by this vulnerability.

Inside the Visitors' Center is a museum, the "Gallery of Space Flight." Among the various exhibits are capsules from the early Mercury, Apollo, and Gemini flights.

The capsules, not much bigger than small cars, are battered and charred from their reentry flights. Consider the courage required to climb into such a craft to be shot into space on the tip of a flaming arrow. If all went well, the capsules fell to earth like crumpled, disregarded toys to be picked up later.

It is not unlike the courage of the first pilots who, knowing that there was no chance if their spindly planes failed, flew without parachutes.

The stars still beckon. For the travelers, the terrible risks are still there. And the courage required is still great.

Photo Opposite
THE SPACE SHUTTLE *CHALLENGER*
JOHN F. KENNEDY SPACE CENTER
FLORIDA
National Aeronautics and Space Administration

MR. NORRIS' IMPROVEMENTS

Mr. Isaac Norris, Speaker of the House of the Royal Province of Pennsylvania, was not impressed with the Royal State House. After all, Philadelphia was one of the prettiest cities in the thirteen colonies. Surely, Norris argued, the people's representatives deserved better than a drafty barn of a building.

For one thing, there were those awful echoes every time someone rose to speak. As a young clerk named Benjamin Franklin once complained, they were ". . . wearisome."

A certain amount of government money had been set aside for the province's general improvement and Speaker Norris set out to make things right.

Soon beautiful new drapes and seat covers helped deaden the awful echo. A splendid new silver inkstand appeared on the Speaker's Table. An elegant new Committee Room was built so that the representatives would have a proper place to relax. Judges blossomed forth in new scarlet robes and white wigs. And a fine new bell tower rose above the city.

As the crowning touch, a massive bell for the tower was commissioned from London's Whitechapel Foundry.

None of this sat very well with the province's citizens who could think of more practical uses for the money like protection against marauding Indians. In one grisly protest, the bodies of three massacred settlers were brought into town and dumped at the State House entrance.

And to top it off, when the new bell arrived from England, it promptly cracked. It was recast but eventually cracked again.

Mr. Norris's improvements made the Royal State House one of the most beautiful buildings in the colonies, and as Independence Hall, in the United States.

The bell was kept, cracks and all. The last time it was actually rung with a clapper was on Washington's birthday in 1846. Today it is known as the Liberty Bell.

A Whoop, a Holler, and Hope

Most western ghost towns were founded on a whoop, a holler, and hope. Like kitchen matches, they flared brightly and briefly. Then the ore ran out or the railroad moved on and the match went out.

Time and vandals have not been kind to the old towns. Usually about all that's left are overgrown foundations and the occasional wink of broken glass in the sagebrush. With each winter's snow, another ancient building collapses into a splintered heap.

But the names are remembered and they spill from the history books with the clatter of an overturned toy box. There was Bogus Thunder and Wildcat Bar and Poker Flat, Shinebone Peak and Git-Up-and-Git.

One wonder if the citizens of Murderer's Bar and Hell's Delight were as ferocious as their towns make them seem. Did the folks who lived in Whiskey Bar and Delirium Tremens drink too much? Were Skunk Gulch and Gospel Swamp as depressing as their names sound?

Towns sometimes took on the names of great cities, hoping it would lend them a cosmopolitan air. It didn't always work. Rome, Texas, all one cabin of it, sent forth no legions. And only tumbleweeds and dust devils dance across the streets of Manhattan, Nevada.

Occasionally local civic-minded types had second thoughts and gave their communities more dignified names. Hangtown, California, didn't conjure up visions of peace and prosperity, so it became Placerville. The citizens of Dog Town, Oregon, were so thrilled when David Hardman opened up a post office, they renamed the town for him.

But then there were the good people of Ground Hog Glory, California, who liked their town's name just fine, thank you. It made you smile.

The town is gone now. But each time we come across the name in a book or on an old map, we smile. And from across a century, the citizens of Ground Hog Glory wink at us.

Photo Opposite
ASHCROFT GHOST TOWN HOTEL
near ASPEN, COLORADO
Ken Dequaine, Photographer

THE FIFES AND DRUMS OF WILLIAMSBURG

The birth of the nation was played out to the music of fifes and drums. British drummers played Major Pitcairn's redcoats onto the green at Lexington. As Washington bitterly retreated south in 1776, his musicians raised the soldiers' spirits with marches and popular tunes. In the terrible battles that followed, the shrill fifes and rumbling drums could be clearly heard above the crack of gunfire and the heavy thump of artillery.

Finally, in 1781, a lone British drummer boy stood on the shattered ramparts of Yorktown and tapped out the sound of surrender. The soldiers went home and the fifes and drums fell silent.

In Williamsburg tradition is as pervasive as the fragrance of dogwood blossoms in the Virginia spring. So it was fitting that the streets of the old city should echo again to the music of its youth.

In 1958 a handful of dedicated enthusiasts founded the Colonial Williamsburg Fife and Drum Corps. The six-holed fifes and the ash drums with their calfskin heads were re-created and the music researched and practiced.

Today the Colonial Williamsburg Fife and Drum Corps has been divided into junior and senior corps and a color guard has been added. In addition to the weekly musters and rehearsals, the corps performs an average of four hundred times a year.

In red coats with blue facings, the musicians march down the green in front of the Governor's Palace. Then, with a sharp wheel to the left, they move smartly up the Duke of Gloucester Street toward the Capitol.

PETERSBURG, VIRGINIA

To know the sorrow and courage of the Civil War, come to Petersburg. But not in May when Virginia is at her loveliest. Come instead in December when the grass is brown and the sky is the color of gun metal and winter-stripped trees stand naked against the horizon.

For ten months the little rebel city on the Appomattox River stood with its back against the wall. For ten months Grant's powerful armies were held at bay.

On a distant ridge, a single lonely chimney stands over the ruins of a fireplace. A farmhouse stood there once. I wonder if the farmer watched his house burn as the first shells landed in his fields.

A photograph taken outside Petersburg shows a young Confederate soldier, a boy really, lying on his back. His face is turned to the afternoon sun. It was spring when the picture was made. The air was so still, a man could hear a woodpecker in a pine grove a quarter mile away. People later remarked how quiet it was, wrote it down in letters home.

He looks as if he might be asleep except for the dried blood running from his nose and across his forehead. In the end Lee commanded an army largely of old men and boys.

One weapon the Union armies used was an ugly brute of a mortar called "The Dictator." It could throw a 200-pound ball two miles into the city. Where it actually landed was anyone's guess.

In Petersburg there was a little girl who had a special doll with a painted china face. And she had a daddy who loved her as much as I love my daughter. I wonder if he rocked her in his arms trying to soothe her when the Dictator was at work.

Today the little doll with the painted china smile is on exhibit in the city's Siege Museum. I don't know what happened to the little girl. I hope she survived. I hope she grew up and had babies of her own.

But I don't know if she did.

THE KACHINAS

When winter comes to the land of the Hopi, the people put on their finest silverwork. Then on certain days, they come together at certain villages. It is the time of *Powamu*, the Bean Dance. It is the time when the Kachinas dance.

To the Hopi Indians of Northern Arizona, the Kachinas come and go with the turning of the seasons. In February *Powamu* announces that spring is near. In July they dance again at *Niman*, just prior to the harvest.

To see the Kachinas is to glimpse into the Hopi soul. Because they are precious to the people's spirit, the dances are not publicized. Outsiders are rarely invited.

However, should a lucky traveler happen upon a dance, they will be made welcome. The Hopi are a private people. But they are also a gracious people.

Each dancer represents a particular Kachina spirit. Eagle Kachina whirls with outstretched wings. Crow Bride Kachina wears her wedding robe and offers a bowl of cornmeal. Squash Kachina enters the plaza painted with the green stripes of his namesake.

The dances are often slow, deliberate, and solemn. Then, suddenly, the solemnity is shattered. The Mud Head Clown Kachinas, with rattles and feathers, have entered the plaza.

Laughter ripples through the crowd as the Mud Heads poke fun at everything and anyone. No one is safe from their needle-sharp satire; not the other Kachinas, not the Hopi, not the visitor.

The Kachinas dance throughout the day. Periodically gifts are distributed , as well as toys for the children, freshly baked loaves of bread, and canned fruit from the trading post.

As one group of Kachinas leaves the plaza, another enters. And so the day goes until twilight. Then, singing a song of farewell, they dance single-file from the plaza.

The people gather their gifts and go home. Soon the biting February winds will give way to warm spring. Then comes the summer harvest. And it will be time for the Kachinas to dance again.

Photo Opposite
HOPI KACHINA EAGLE DOLL
Frederick R. Mollner, Photographer

BLAINE! BLAINE! JAMES G. BLAINE!

L et's face it: Americans love a winner. True, we cheer for the underdog. But winners get into halls of fame and have movies made about them and babies named for them.

Which makes the governor's mansion in Augusta, Maine, all the more special. You see, it was once the home of a gentleman named James G. Blaine.

As a politician Mr. Blaine racked up some pretty fair successes. These, however, did not include becoming president of the United States. Not that he didn't give it his best shot.

In 1876 he tried to run for president. But the Republicans refused to nominate him.

In 1880 he tried again. They still refused to nominate him.

In 1884 he tried again. This time the Republicans gave in and nominated him. He promptly lost the election.

There was a snappy little ditty at the time, popular with Democrats and jump ropers:

Blaine! Blaine! James G. Blaine!
Continental liar from the state of Maine!

Now when it comes down to it, Blaine was no worse than anybody else in the rough-and-tumble world of nineteenth-century politics. And that's not the point anyway.

The point is that he gave it his best shot. And when they knocked him down, he got up and took another shot. And another.

So the next time you're in Augusta, stop by the tidy white mansion with the flag out front on State Street. Inside, you can get a free pamphlet on the state of Maine and see the silver service from the battleship *Maine*.

And when you see the portrait of James G. Blaine, smile. He didn't get the big prize, but it's nice to see someone remembered who lost with such dash.

I n the humid Louisiana night, a small crowd gathers on New Orleans' St. Peter's Street. A wrought-iron gate swings open quietly and they file into an old building stained by the years. Since 1961 it has been the home of the New Orleans Preservation Hall Jazz Band.

The musicians are in their 70s and 80s, their faces creased by time. They play jazz. It's that simple. Real jazz.

Jazz as strident as a field holler, as soft as sweet molasses slipping off a spoon. The kind of jazz heard around Storyville back when it was still called "jass." The kind of jazz Bunk Johnson and Kid Ory and Jelly Roll Morton played. And King Oliver and his Creole Jazz Band. It was Oliver who took in a ragman named Louis "Satchmo" Armstrong who wanted to play the trumpet.

Jazz was born in New Orleans, but at first the parent refused to accept its child. "Jazz," sniffed one local writer in 1918, "is a manifestation of a low streak in man's taste. Although New Orleans has been called its birthplace . . . we do not recognize parenthood."

But the syncopated beat was carried on up the Mississippi into the heartland of America, to Chicago and St. Louis who added their touches. Then east to New York and west to San Francisco's North Beach where they play it as cool as a bay fog.

At the Preservation Hall the evening is winding down. There will be a rambunctious rendition of "When the Saints Go Marching In." And then maybe something a little more gentle, like "Nearer My God to Thee," the clarinet stretching out the notes like salt-water taffy. Then they'll send everybody out the door with "Didn't He Ramble."

"Didn't he ramble, didn't he ramble,
Rambled till the butcher cut him down."
That's jazz. Oh, yes.

Concern for Mr. Dunham

As the centuries pass, the Pilgrims become more and more enshrouded in myth. There is the gloomy schoolbook Pilgrim: a pale pinched face peering out from beneath a big black hat with silver buckles. And there is the greeting card Pilgrim cheerfully slicing up a Thanksgiving turkey for his Indian guests.

But when one opens up the old books, a different Pilgrim emerges from the ornate handwriting with its archaic spelling. This Pilgrim is different from the popular images, yet not so different from us. On the brown pages of the Plymouth Church Records are recorded their fears and joys and concerns.

In 1681 the Rev. John Cotton wrote of his concern for Samuel Dunham. Something was bothering Dunham. Maybe he was homesick for the Old World left behind. Or maybe he suffered some terrible loss. We'll never know.

But whatever it was, Samuel Dunham had found solace in liquor. For a while he stopped drinking but, as Rev. Cotton sadly recorded, he, ". . . formerly failing by intemperence, was againe overtaken in the same kinde."

The church elders tried to reach out to Dunham, offering to meet privately with him. Dunham would have none of it. "He came not to the meeting," wrote Cotton, "and though sent for, came not." Finally Dunham was reluctantly banished, "excommunicated by the Elder in the name of the church."

There is a postscript in the story of Samuel Dunham. In the Plymouth Church Record, it is noted that Mr. Dunham ". . . upon his manifestation of repentence was reconciled to the church."

And so, emerging from the ancient pages are not cardboard images but people who knew the same joys and failings we do, including a concerned minister and a troubled man who eventually found peace.

THE PIG AND THE POTATO PATCH

Deep in the Pacific Northwest where the San Juan Islands lie like emeralds flung across the sea is a monument to a silly war. It is known to history as the Pig War, after its only casualty.

By 1846 the boundary between Canada and the United States had been agreed upon. That is, except for the nagging question of just who owned the lush San Juan Islands in northern Puget Sound. While Washington and London exchanged diplomatic notes, settlers from both sides moved into the islands.

Then in 1859 on San Juan Island, an English pig bumbled into an American potato patch. The farmer, in defense of his potatoes, shot the intruder. Unfortunately, the deceased belonged to the local English peace officer, who tried to haul the American into court in Victoria.

The American refused to go and rallied his friends to stand behind him. The Englishman did likewise. The Americans, refusing to be intimidated, called for help. Soon a company of U.S. soldiers arrived.

The British announced they weren't about to be intimidated either. Three warships dropped anchor and began landing Royal Marines. The U.S. promptly sent in more troops, along with the commanding general of the army.

For a while, the opposing armies glowered at each other from opposite ends of the island. Then, as misty winter gave way to spring, tensions settled. For twelve years, the English occupied one half of the island while the Americans held the other.

Everybody got along splendidly. The two armies held athletic contests and the generals threw parties for each other. Bored soldiers passed the time watching killer whales slice through Puget Sound's chilly gray waters.

Eventually the matter was settled. Both sides, feeling a bit foolish about the whole thing, broke camp and went home.

Today the American camp is a pleasant park with picnic tables and walking trails. The English camp, also a park, has a wooden blockhouse at the edge of the water. The gun that started it all ended up in a museum. And the only casualty was made into sausages.

DEATH VALLEY NATIONAL MONUMENT
CALIFORNIA
Josef Muench, Photographer

ROADS TO NATURAL FORMATIONS

ICEBERG LAKE

igh in the mountains of Montana's Glacier National Park is a small, lovely legacy of the ice age. It is a sliver of turquoise water called Iceberg Lake. As lakes go, it is not large, perhaps 100 square acres.

However, the lake is cold. Even in July and August, when the sun hangs hot in the sky, small icebergs bob in the water. Cleaved off of a wall of glistening ice at the head of the lake, they will not melt for days.

Iceberg Lake fills a depression left eons ago when a shimmering river of ice moved through the mountains. Today, rocks ground into powder by the relentless glacier give the water an opaque look.

The lake, an easy six-mile hike from the nearest hotel, is popular with visitors. Children hesitantly poke their fingers into the water and quickly draw them back with a shiver. Fathers, tongues firmly in cheek, explain that the water is so cold that trout can survive only by growing little fur coats.

Far above the lake, small patches of white (like bits of unmelted snow) dot steep cliffsides. It is only when the patches move that the visitor realizes they are mountain goats. Leaping nimbly from crag to crag, white fur stark against the gray rock, the aloof animals ignore the people below.

Safe in their high domain, the mountain goats gambol among the precipices and sharp ridges. Occasionally rocks are dislodged and fall, ricocheting off the sheer granite walls until they land hundreds of feet below.

NIAGARA FALLS

I n 1678 French missionary Louis Hennepin stumbled through thick forests to stand thunderstruck on the bank of the Niagara River. The ground shook beneath him as the river threw itself from a cliff in a great waterfall. Amid the deafening roar, clouds of mist boiled into the sky.

When Hennepin returned to civilization, he announced that the falls called Niagara fell six hundred feet to their base! A later eyewitness report was just as certain the falls were even higher: eight hundred feet high.

In fact, Niagara Falls is a little over 180 feet tall at its highest point. The water thunders downward at an average 200,000 cubic feet per second. The sheer volume of rushing water is so great that the limestone precipice crumbles under it at about a foot a year.

Within a few years of its discovery, Niagara Falls was a major tourist attraction. As early as 1837, locals were complaining that along with the tourists came an army of ". . . cabmen, storekeepers, sight showers, and hotel keepers, all working to plunder."

Meanwhile, the falls themselves have been assaulted by all sorts of indignities. In 1827 an aging schooner was shoved over the falls and smashed to splinters on the rocks below. Newspapers at the time said it was the highlight of the tourist season.

In 1901 a lady named Annie Edwards crawled into a barrel and went tumbling over the falls. Hauled battered and bleeding from the water, she sputtered that no one "ought ever to do that again!"

Of course Ms. Edwards had hardly dried out before the first challenger went rolling off the edge. Yet, through it all, Niagara Falls has retained all the majesty and power that transfixed Louis Hennepin so long ago.

THE DAY PELE TREMBLED

There is a terrible beauty in the volcano of Kilauea on the island of Hawaii. Within its craters seethes a fearsome lake of tortured earth split by lava and vented by hissing steam. Visitors, peering over the edge, are assaulted by the sting of sulfur. Here, say old Hawaiians, was the dwelling place of Pele, Mother of Volcanoes.

They feared her wrath as the earth trembled and her hot blood spewed forth to burn the land. Deep within her mountain, she roared her defiance, even as the missionaries preached against her.

So it fell to a lone Hawaiian woman to do what the missionaries could not. Her name was Kapiolani and this is how she banished Pele into the myths of ancient Hawaii.

She was born an *alii*, a noble, and became renowned for her good works as a Christian. But she was distressed at the grip of fear with which Pele held many Hawaiians. To break that grip, Kapiolani knew she would have to defy Pele. In December 1824, with a few loyal friends, Kapiolani climbed the burning mountain of Kilauea.

Midway she was stopped by an old woman, a high priestess of Pele. Dark eyes glittering, the priestess muttered dire warnings. Kapiolani continued on to the lip of the volcano.

Below her, the earth heaved and flames spilled into the air. Standing straight and tall, she faced the terrible heat. She denounced Pele and prayed. Then, in a clear voice, she sang a hymn.

From the pit came only the growling of lava and clouds of foul-smelling gas.

Kapiolani turned and came down the mountain. Quickly the news spread. Confronted by the Christian God, Pele had not lashed out but only trembled in her pit!

The missionary flocks swelled. And for many years visitors were shown where Kapiolani had stood until, at last, this spot, too, crumbled into the pit.

Photo Opposite
VOLCANO KILAUEA
HAWAII VOLCANOES NATIONAL PARK
HAWAII
Bob Seibert, Photographer

TIJUANA RIVER ESTUARY

In the southwest corner of the United States, the Tijuana River meanders across the border from Mexico's brown hills. Seemingly in no hurry to reach the sea, it wanders the Tijuana River Valley for several miles before spilling into the Pacific.

Ocean tides, nudged by the moon, flow into the low valley marshlands. The salt and fresh water merge and the resulting estuary nourishes a rich and vibrant little world.

The mood and personality of the estuary change with the ebb and flow of the tides. And with the seasons. With the dry southern California summer, the river slows to a murky trickle and disappears into the sand. A few months later, swollen with winter rain, the river emerges to fill the channel.

And with winter come the great migrations of birds. They arrive in vast numbers to rest after the long flight south and to warm themselves in the mild winter sun. Researchers have counted over three hundred species of birds in the estuary.

The plants of the marsh are as hardy as their names suggest: salt grass, alkali heath, and pickleweed. In the dry and salty coastal sand dunes, sand verbena plants send tap roots deep into the dune for water. And somehow, life not only perseveres but flourishes.

Not so long ago, the estuary, neglected and abused, was in danger. But the sea lavender plants and the sandpipers and fiddler crabs had friends.

In the nearby little coastal town of Imperial Beach, volunteers got together and started the Southwest Wetlands Interpretive Association. Federal and California State agencies joined forces.

Today the estuary, now officially the Tijuana River National Estuarine Research Reserve, is lovingly protected. Trash has been cleared away and the dunes are being reseeded. Ground has been broken for a Visitors' Center. And once again it is safe for the Savannah sparrow to make its nest in the pickleweed.

Photo Opposite
AMERICAN AVOCET
TIJUANA RIVER ESTUARINE RESEARCH RESERVE,
CALIFORNIA
Phillip C. Roullard, Photographer

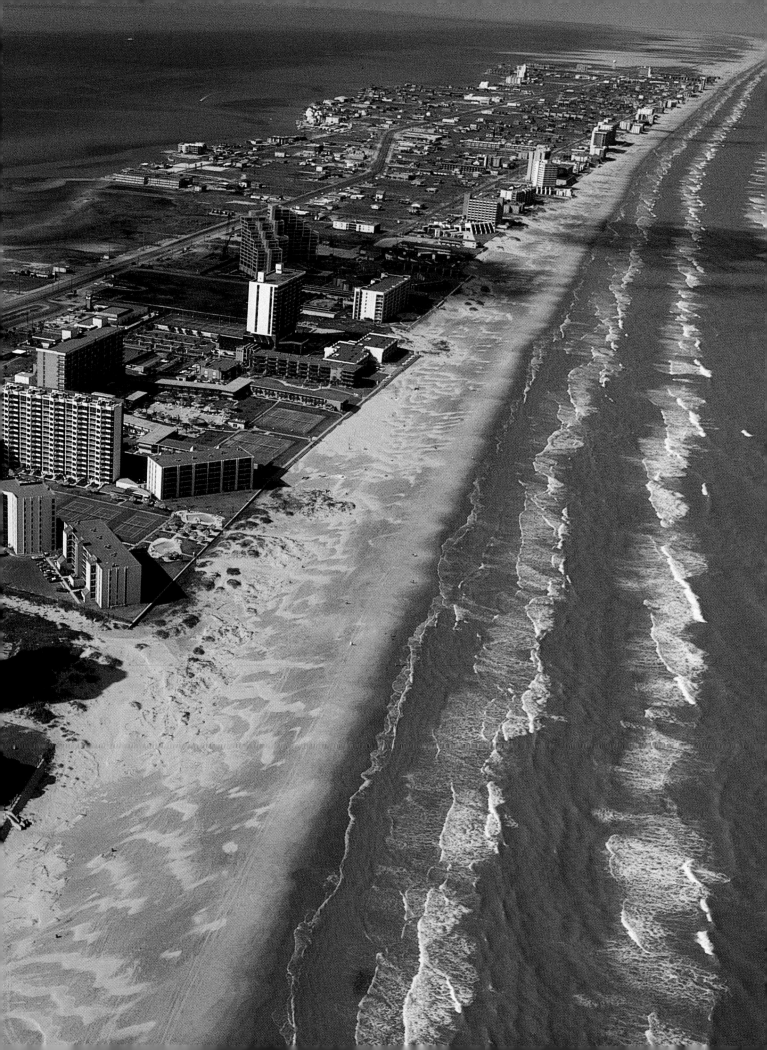

PADRE ISLAND NATIONAL SEASHORE

Padre Island National Seashore is the kind of place map makers have nightmares about. An ever-shifting sandbar, it stretches like a thin snake eighty-odd miles along the south Texas coast. Separated from the mainland by the Laguna Madre, it is usually no more than three or four miles wide at any time.

Winds constantly rearrange carefully noted dunes, and waves fill in or eat away beaches at whim. Storms from the Gulf of Mexico lash at the shore, cutting a new channel here, filling in an old one there.

And with the morning calm come the beachcombers. In addition to its spectacular natural beauty, Padre Island National Seashore is the holy grail of beachcombing. Most of the time the beachcombers have to be content with sea shells or interesting bits of debris tossed up on the sand.

But once in a great while, the sand and the tide are generous. And sharp eyes discern a bit of metal in the otherwise flawless white sand. Maybe it's a Union Army belt buckle or a fistfull of bullets from one of the Civil War camps.

Or maybe it's a gold doubloon or scarlet ruby winking in the sun. After all, a terrible storm in 1553 hurled an entire Spanish treasure fleet against the island.

And watch out for a large round stone. Jean Lafitte's pirates sheltered their ships in the Laguna Madre. And, the story goes, they buried a great treasure beneath a millstone.

But be prepared to do a lot of walking in soft sand that would wear out Lawrence of Arabia. For a few miles there is paved road. After that you are on your own with the dunes and the wind and the sea gulls wheeling high in the blue sky.

SECRET BENEATH THE EARTH

For uncounted centuries the earth kept its secret deep beneath the Texas hill country. Then one day in 1960, four spelunkers, cave explorers, showed up at the Natural Bridge Ranch a few miles outside of San Antonio. They wanted to explore around the underground passages near the natural limestone bridge for which the ranch is named.

Wriggling into one of the tight passages, the explorers felt a faint draft of cool air. Chipping their way downward, they emerged into a fantastic wonderland of chambers and corridors.

Stalactites hung from the ceiling, oozing downward, growing an inch with each passing century. Stalagmites spiraled upward from the cave floor. Pools of water that have never felt the ripple of the wind stood clear as crystal and still as glass.

The explorers found that other men had penetrated the caves' darkness before them. Indian spearpoints lay on the cave floor. Nearby was the jawbone of a species of bear not seen on the Texas plains for 8,000 years.

On the Natural Bridge Ranch, the work of raising livestock on a 2,200-acre spread goes on. Cattle graze contentedly on the range and there are sheep and goats. But now the ranch receives visitors from all over the world who have come to see the marvels below.

The caverns have been disturbed as little as possible. But unlike the 1960 explorers, today's visitors do not have to wriggle their way through twisting passageways. Instead, guided tours are led down comfortable, well-lit paths.

Passing over Purgatory Creek and through a stone Sherwood Forest, guests enter the 350-foot-long Hall of the Mountain King. All about, sculptured stone towers cast their shapes against the walls.

Usually the only sound in the caverns they hear is the soft distant drip of water as the patient work of centuries goes on. But after a rainstorm on the surface, there is the faint sound of a swollen river rushing far below.

Clearly the Natural Bridge Caverns have not given up all their secrets.

MIRACLE OF THE ANZA-BORREGO

California's Anza-Borrego Desert State Park sprawls across a half million rugged acres scoured by rocky washes and narrow, winding gorges. It is named for Juan Bautista de Anza who trudged across the desolate landscape in the name of his Spanish king in 1774. And for the *borrego*, which is Spanish for the desert bighorn sheep who nimbly dance across its foothill boulders.

It is a land with a long memory. There are mysterious images on the desert floor carved by Cahuilla Indians a millenium ago. And there are the ruts from stagecoach wheels.

Like all deserts it has no mercy for the foolish. In the shimmering heat of summer, just touching the sand can bring a blister. With winter come lower temperatures and a meager three or four inches of rain.

Spring is when the Anza-Borrego is at its mildest. And the desert celebrates with a miracle. For a few short weeks, the hard scrabble floor is splashed with color as the wildflowers bloom.

Somber beavertail cactus suddenly blossoms forth with gaudy purple flowers. Pale chicory softens desert scrub. Delicate stalks of flowers rise from spikey Mojave yucca. Tiny scarlet blossoms crown tall spidery ocotillo branches.

For an all too short while, the desert is a living artist's palette of colors. Then, as spring slides into summer, the sun grows hot and angry. The fragile blossoms wither. But eventually the seasons will turn and summer will surrender to fall and winter. And then spring will come and the desert will again be splashed with color.

WUPATKI RUIN
WUPATKI NATIONAL MONUMENT
ARIZONA
Dick Dietrich Photography

ROADS TO STRUCTURES

SHINING BEACONS

There is something wonderfully bold about lighthouses. They are declarations to the sea that, while we respect and fear it, we will not be intimidated.

Lighthouses have been built where they have no right to be. They perch on cliffs and cling to rocks while the waves wash over them. They come in all shapes and sizes, from North Carolina's soaring candy-striped Cape Hatteras to the fire-engine red square tower of Michigan's Holland Harbor.

Some are so isolated that keepers were all but driven mad with loneliness. Others blink within rowing distance of great cities. Jeffries Hook Lighthouse, for example, is literally in the shadow of New York City's George Washington Bridge.

The men and women who manned the lighthouses often did so at the risk of their lives. Biscayne Bay's Cape Florida Light was attacked and burned by Seminole Indians. Alaska's Scotch Cape Light was obliterated by a tidal wave.

Today some of the old lighthouses are dark, technological dinosaurs no longer needed. Others still cast their lights in sweeping arcs across the water. But the keepers have been replaced by computers and automated machinery.

Fortunately for those who love lighthouses, many of the older ones have been preserved. Some have found new lives as hotels or bed and breakfast inns. Others, like New York's Fire Island Lighthouse or New Jersey's Barnegat Light, are museums.

One by one the lighthouses have been modernized or replaced. But they will never disappear from our coasts. Not as long as fog shrouds the rocks or there is an angry wind to lash the sea.

THE TEXTILE MILLS OF NEW ENGLAND

Once these old buildings were filled with the rumble of machinery. Now they stand silent, their brick facades mirrored in the streams that helped power their machines. Even the footsteps of an occasional visitor are swallowed by the heavy walls.

From these New England textile mills came the bright cottons that Yankee clippers carried to the ends of the earth. Came also were the blue woolen uniforms to clothe the Union army.

Today the massive, dusty machinery with its great wheels and iron gears seems embarassingly quaint. And, yes, the pay was often wretched and the hours long, and there was child labor.

But the mills were the muscles of an industrial revolution that saw the United States mature into a great power. And many an immigrant's dreams became reality thanks to a mill paycheck.

For reasons like these, and because the buildings themselves are handsome and well crafted, there are several mills still in existence.

Some have found new life in new uses. The Amoskeag Mill, its graceful walls curving along New Hampshire's Merrimack River, houses offices and high-tech companies.

Here and there, an old mill has been preserved as a museum. One of the most beautiful is the Slater Mill on the banks of the Blackstone River in Pawtucket, Rhode Island. Its red-faced building trimmed in white and mounted by an elegant cupola make it appear more statehouse than factory.

For the neglected and empty mills, the future need not always be bleak. Growing numbers of people appreciate them not only for their beauty but for what they represent. Within their strong walls is a part of our American heritage.

CHARLES W. MORGAN

Broad-beamed and squared off, she is no greyhound of the seas. But on the sturdy decks of ships like the *Charles W. Morgan*, fortunes were made. For she was a Yankee whaler.

She was built by Jethro and Zachariah Hillman of solid New England timber and launched at New Bedford in July 1841. Once she had hundreds of sisters. Whalers, it was said, were built by the mile and sawed off as needed.

Now there is only one. The *Charles W. Morgan* is the last wooden New Bedford whaler. For nearly a century she ranged the seven seas, brawling her way around Cape Horn to the Pacific whaling grounds. Now she tugs gently at her mooring lines at Mystic Seaport, Connecticut.

She carried four whaleboats suspended from her sides. When her lookouts spotted a whale, the boats were quickly away, harpooner at each bow.

When the harpoon was driven home, the whale might lash out with his flukes, splintering the boat. Or he might dive deep beneath the surface. When he finally tired, a whaler's lance finished him and the great beast's body was towed back to the *Morgan*.

There the whale was cut up and rendered into oil. Thick black smoke boiled into the air while sea gulls wheeled high in the sky.

Today the huge iron rendering kettles are cold. A museum, the *Morgan*'s decks are spanking clean, her ropes neatly coiled. She looks as she must have looked when she first stood out to sea, her black hull glistening in the sun and the wind filling her sails.

DESERT VIEW TOWER

Highway eight winds through the boulder-strewn Jacumba Mountains along the California-Mexico border. One end stops just short of the Pacific Ocean, the other wanders off into the Arizona Desert.

For a half century, travelers driving up from the frying pan of the Imperial Valley have stopped to cool their radiators at the Desert View Tower. For miles the tower stands out on the horizon like a beckoning lighthouse.

For the weary driver there are bathrooms and a cool drink and a bit of shade. There is a wonderfully rambling museum crammed with this and that from spinning wheels to scrimshaw. And there is the view.

Seen from the tower's rocky perch, the desert floor is spread out in all its stark beauty. In the distance the blue puddle of the Salton Sea dances in the shimmering heat like a mirage. The Chocolate Mountains cast their shadows across bleached-bone sand. A pale patch on the far horizon marks shifting dunes along the Colorado River.

Visitors peer through binoculars and take a few snapshots. Some take time to chat with the pleasant people who run the tower, maybe buy a postcard or two.

By sunset the last of the dusty cars has pulled out of the driveway back onto the highway. The boulders around the tower are busy with desert creatures emerging into the cool evening. Before long, stars will fill the dark sky like diamond dust flung across blue velvet.

WHEN HOLLYWOOD WAS A LITTLE FARM TOWN

As barns go, it isn't much. A small yellow building, it sits in a little park just across from the Hollywood Bowl. It's been moved several times. Originally it was a few mile down the road at the corner of Vine and Selma. Then it had horses in it.

That was back when Hollywood was a little farm town just outside Los Angeles. In 1913 a young easterner named Cecil B. DeMille rented the barn. He was making a movie and needed a place to work that didn't cost too much.

The movie was a ripsnorter of a western called "The Squaw Man." It was made for a total cost of $15,000. At a dime a ticket at the box office, "The Squaw Man" earned over $225,000, and life in Hollywood was never the same again.

Vamps vamped, villians villified, and cream pies flew through the air. Griffith Park rang to the gunfire of movie cowboys. Hollywood's tidy little homes and farms and churches gave way to backlots with Moorish minarets and Norman castles.

Today Hollywood's glamour is pretty threadbare. Most of the studios pulled out long ago and moved up the road to Burbank.

But thanks to a group of volunteers called Hollwood Heritage Inc., you can see where it all started. The barn, now called the Hollywood Studio Museum, is a treasure trove of film artifacts.

The old Underwood typewriter used to type up "The Squaw Man" shooting script sits on a table. A camera used by Charlie Chaplin is there, along with one of Gloria Swanson's gowns. Pirate ship models from a Douglas Fairbanks swashbuckler are there and so is Pola Negri's stool. You can still read where DeMille had "Miss Negri only" painted on the wood.

They're all there in the little barn, memories from when movies were in their infancy and still fun to make, when scripts were tapped out on typewriters, and being a star meant getting your own footstool.

THE BELLS STILL RING OUT

T wenty-one missions, each a hard day's ride from the next, march up the length of California. Bent under the weight of years, they are gentle, almost humble buildings now, filled with the dust of time. But during the golden decades of Spain's glory, their adobe walls marked the edge of a mighty empire.

The south is anchored by San Diego de Alcala, founded in 1769. The once-surrounding fields and pastures were long ago swallowed up by the bustling, modern city of San Diego. But the ancient mission bells still ring out each day to call the faithful.

Three weeks' march north is San Francisco de Solano, founded in 1823. More modest than its sisters, Solano was built in the twilight of the mission era.

The missions today are tranquil places of carefully tended gardens and buildings that whisper of the past. But once they hummed with activity as vast herds of cattle dotted the brown hills and bountiful crops were harvested in the fields and orchards. In workshops and schools, thousands of Indian coverts learned to make their way in the strange new world suddenly thrust upon them.

The mission system has been frequently criticized and not without reason. Along with new ways, the missions also brought new sicknesses, and Indian populations were decimated. And there were missionaries who, in their zeal to teach, erased proud heritages.

Still, one cannot help but admire those who so long ago came to a raw and desolate frontier and said, "Here there shall be places of learning, here there shall be order and peace."

SOUTH PEACHAM, VERMONT
Fred Sieb, Photographer

122

ROADS DOWN COUNTRY LANES

PARTICULARLY THE SPLENDID FISHING

President Calvin Coolidge was feeling very proud of himself. Wearing rubber boots, he stood in the chill waters of South Dakota's Squaw Creek. Whipping his fishing pole over his head in graceful arcs, he sent his fly licking across the stream. Time after time, the trout snapped hungrily at his lure.

South Dakota Governor Carl Gunderson stood nearby and smiled approvingly. The governor had invited President Coolidge to come to the Black Hills and vacation at the state's game lodge. It was the summer of 1927 and the weather was glorious.

The president's fishing creel was soon full and he splashed happily ashore. That night there would be a fine feast at the lodge.

Of course, Coolidge had no way of knowing that his sudden great fishing skill was due to a bit of sleight of hand. It seems Squaw Creek had been fenced off upstream, and this section was stocked with trout trucked in from the state fish hatchery at Spearfish. Trout fattened on ground meat. Trout who were now very hungry.

What Calvin Coolidge didn't know was that by the time he went fishing, those trout would have gone after a bent safety pin!

But it didn't matter. Soon the eyes and ears of the nation would be focused on South Dakota, and Governor Gunderson was determined to have a very happy president on hand.

A few days later, hundreds of people stood on a mountain deep in the Black Hills. Among them were reporters from every major newspaper.

Coolidge, full of praise for South Dakota, made a ringing speech of dedication. Gesturing at the rugged granite around him, he said that soon a memorial would rise here ". . . for all time."

As they walked back down the mountain, Coolidge thanked Gunderson for a wonderful time, particularly the splendid fishing. Behind them, work began in earnest on the Mount Rushmore National Memorial.

Photo Opposite
SPLENDID FISHING
David Stoeckleir/The Stock Solution

HANCOCK SHAKER VILLAGE

They called themselves the United Society of Believers in Christ's Second Appearing. We know them as Shakers.

At their peak in the 1840s, over 5,000 Shakers lived in eighteen communities. The sound of their religious fervor filled their meeting houses and rolled across their carefully tended pastures.

Now the meeting houses are silent. The last Shakers, a handful of frail, elderly women, serenely await the passing of their faith. It is all as founder Mother Anne predicted long ago, even as she laid the foundations of Shakerism.

The Shakers believed in efficiency and welcomed new ways to lighten the work load. The clothespin, flat broom, and circular saw are Shaker creations, along with the threshing machine and screw propeller.

Their buildings and furnishings are marked with a special grace and balance. Even as simple a thing as a chair was crafted with such a slim elegance that, to paraphrase Thomas Merton, it seemed as if an angel might come and sit on it.

The Hancock Shaker village nestles in the rolling, green velvet hills of eastern Massachusetts near Pittsfield. No Shakers have lived in the village since 1960. Today it has been lovingly restored as a testament of the Shaker way of life.

The various workshops, barns, and dwellings do not disrupt the harmony of nature but complement it. Sometimes even the pasture fence seems to bend to the contours of the land like water seeking a natural course.

At the same time, there is an austere beauty in the strict symmetry of the buildings. To the Shakers, order and simplicity were benchmarks to guide one's days, like the garden you pass through as you walk up the path into the village.

Precisely laid out, the garden is bright with blooming flowers. But flowers meant seeds to be packaged and sold and herbs to be ground into medicines. It is a Shaker garden. It is lovely, but above all, it is useful and efficient.

Photo Opposite
HANCOCK SHAKER VILLAGE
MASSACHUSETTS
Howard Karger/New England Stock Photo

BRANDING TIME

The day began with pickup trucks poking their way through the blue Wyoming dawn down to the cattle pens. It's cold, bitterroot cold; enough that the cowboys welcome a hot cup of coffee as much to warm their hands around as to drink. Someone tunes in a country music station on the radio, and soon a female voice is bemoaning her lost love.

Once there were long drives down from the high country or up to the railhead, but all that is past now. Today small planes patrol distant ranch boundaries while four-wheel-drive trucks grind their way over sage-covered hills. But for the cowboy, the long hours are still there and the work is still bone-hard.

It's branding time; and by mid-morning the air is filled with dust and men's voices and the bawling of calves. One after another the calves are cut out from the herd into chutes. The chutes narrow and the calves find themselves held firm in a final squeeze chute.

The men operating the chute work with practiced efficiency as each calf is branded and vaccinated in less than a minute. A crack crew can process fifty to sixty animals in an hour. The chute is opened and the calf bolts free to rejoin the herd. Before the day is done, several hundred cattle will pass through the chute.

With evening the men climb into trucks for the long haul back to the ranch headquarters. They are among the last of their breed. Today there are fewer than a thousand full-time working cowboys in America. Behind them a full moon climbs into the eastern sky like a double eagle twenty-dollar gold piece. But most of the cowboys are too exhausted to notice or care.

PERSEVERENCE IN A HARD LAND

Deep in the Great Smoky Mountains is a monument to a people's perseverence and hard labor. It is a simple log farmhouse. Nearby are such mundane farm structures as a chicken house, corn crib, and pig pen. And there is a meat house where large hams coated with salt from a lick once hung in neat rows.

Life for the nineteenth-century farmers of North Carolina's Oconaluftee Valley was filled with loneliness and drudgery. The surrounding spruce and hemlock forests were beautiful, but the soil was not particularly bountiful. To supplement their meager harvests, many small farmers fell back on trapping and hunting.

In their isolation, the mountaineers became self-sufficient and asked little of the outside world. What they could not buy, they made. Often it was hardest on the women, who put in long mind-numbing days of molding candles, pouring soap, grinding meal, and spinning thread.

Changes came slowly in the remoteness of the mounains. Well into the twentieth century, there were isolated places in the Oconaluftee Valley where frontier ways lived on.

But in time the isolation was shattered by logging companies who coveted the lush forests. In 1934 Congress authorized the Great Smoky Mountains National Park. Logging ceased, but the mountains had already been stripped of sixty percent of their trees, and the world of the mountaineer farmer had changed forever.

But their crafts and skills, along with the pride and dignity of their self-sufficiency, are reproduced at the park's Oconaluftee Visitors' Center. In a simple pioneer farmstead is recalled the strength of a people who persevered in a beautiful but hard land.

RAIN ON THE PRAIRIES

Deep in the heart of the Great Plains, even the rivers are mild-mannered. The North Platte, the Missouri, and the Arkansas wind leisurely through rolling hills and flat plains on their way to the distant Gulf of Mexico. Cottonwoods shade their banks and the hillsides are speckled with primroses and bluebonnets. Cattle graze in pastures of lush prairie grass.

Small towns connected by a network of county rural roads dot the map. There are still ranches scattered around, but mostly the people are farmers. Spring sees the first thunderstorms. The first warning comes when the north sky turns leaden and angry and a wind begins to whip the grass. Spider tracings of white light crackle across the sky as lightning lashes the horizon. For a micro-second the landscape lights up as brightly as if a flashgun had gone off. A moment later the bass-drum rumble of thunder rolls across the plains.

Flatland thunderstorms are taken seriously. Radio and television interrupt their programs for updates from the National Weather Service.

When the rain does come, it is heavy and hard. As if ripped open by the lightning, the sky empties itself on the land. Automobiles seek the safety of highway overpasses in case of hail which can crack a windshield like a rock dropped from the sky.

Then, almost as abruptly as it started, the rain stops and the wind tapers off. The storm moves on. For a little while the rivers run heavy like skittish colts and then settle down.

HAD I KNOWN

Recently I was in an antique shop when I came across an old friend. There in a hutch, between the French porcelain and a Georgian silver bowl, was a Soldier of the Queen.

He was a little over two inches tall, made of lead and, though flecks of paint were missing, his jacket was still a proud scarlet.

Made by a company called Britains, he had originally been part of a squad of toy soldiers in a long narrow box. When I saw him, memories of warm afternoons and a backyard dirt pile swept over me. I had a set of soldiers just like him and they fought many a glorious battle.

That is, except for the dashing young officer with his silver sword. As he was leading his first charge, my dog ran off with him and he was never seen again. A thousand years from now, an archeologist digging in what was once a west Seattle backyard will find him and he will end up labled "Ceremonial Object" in a museum.

There is something disconcerting about finding a toy from one's childhood in an antique shop. I asked the clerk what other antique toys they might have.

She replied sadly that antique toys are fairly rare. Mass-produced toys weren't common until the nineteenth century and not all that many survived their young owners. Among those she showed me were a cast-iron fire engine from the 1890s, a china-head doll from around 1880, and a splendid wind-up tin battleship from around 1910. I also saw a small tin log cabin.

"Ah, yes," she said, "that's what we call a nostalgia item. Once it held Log Cabin Syrup."

I remember those little tin log cabins. And had I known what they sell for today, I certainly would have eaten a lot more pancakes.

IOWA FARM COUNTRY

Deep in Iowa's farm country, fields of wheat stretch to the horizon in a golden, shimmering sea. But the chances are good that no loaves of bread will come from it. Like the fields of soybeans and corn, much of it will become feed for livestock.

You know you're in farm country when the news spends more time talking about the weather than sports. A change in the weather can spell life or death for a crop and sometimes a farm.

Driving down Main Street in a farm town, the traveler passes small coffee shops. By mid-morning, farmers, faces creased by sun and wind, start drifting in for coffee and a doughnut. Most wear billed caps called "Gimmie Hats."

The name comes from the time when agricultural supply firms gave them away free as advertising.

For a farmer, mid-morning means mid-day and time for a break. If you've fields to tend, you roll the tractor out of the barn at first light. On most dairies first milking comes at about 5:30 A.M. before the frost has melted into dew.

Like parents everywhere, farmers talk about their children. An Iowa farm child can tell you the make of a tractor on the horizon by its color. Green, for example, means it's a John Deere; whereas red identifies an old International Harvester. Bright yellow, it's a Caterpillar.

Inevitably the talk turns to weather. They hope for good drying weather when the soil is dry yet still moist enough for good planting. And they look forward to late spring when the last snow has drifted across the fields and planting time is near. It is a time of renewal.

About noon they break up to take care of errands in town. Usually this means a trip to the store or a stop at the bank or the county agent's office. Then, one by one, the dusty pickups disappear down the county roads on their way back to the fields.

Photo Opposite
GOLDEN GRAIN
Colour Library International

AMERICA A LA CARTE

As a boy in the Pacific Northwest, I dug clams from the Puget Sound beaches pretty much as I imagined Florida kids plucked oranges from backyard trees. Other than that I never gave much thought to regional food.

Then I came to California, where I discovered Mexican food and learned that coleslaw is not really a salad.

When I started travel writing, well-meaning friends warned me about regional food. I was advised to be especially wary of southern food. First they fry it senseless, I was told, and if that doesn't kill it, they drown it in gummy white gravy.

A southern colleague assured me those were all base Yankee lies. Of course, he also calls the Civil War "the War of Northern Aggression."

Since then I have learned that there is life after chicken-fried steak in Texas and that Virginians make biscuits the way God intended them to be made. A North Carolina relative introduced me to Brunswick Stew. He was a little apologetic since it didn't contain real squirrel meat, but I thought it was terrific.

The fun is in the discovery. In Manhattan I was taken to dinner in an elegant restaurant with tassels on the menu. But later on the sidewalk outside my hotel, I found a pushcart with the most wonderful pretzels, big and warm and soft.

Oh, there have been setbacks, like the passage into Texan manhood that requires eating chili seasoned with hot coals plucked from the fires of hell.

I'll admit that southern barbecue is pretty good; but that luau on Ohau when they pried the hot stones off the *imu*, the underground oven, was wonderful.

The *kulua* pork had been slowly roasted for hours. And when the pit was finally opened, the smell was so good, even the pig was smiling.

MT. SHASTA
WEED, CALIFORNIA
McKinney/H. Armstrong Roberts, Inc.

ROADS TO WILDLIFE

PRAIRIE DOG TOWN

Not so long ago on the Great Plains, vast cities with millions of inhabitants sprawled across the land. Their neighborhoods were interconnected by a system of tunnels that would put the New York subway system to shame.

The architects of these communities were small furry rodents dubbed *petit chien*, little dog, by early French explorers. Later settlers called them "barking squirrels." Wildlife experts estimate that once the grasslands teemed with billions of them.

They are, of course, the prairie dog. There are fewer now. For a century they have been assaulted by pest control, plagues, and hunters.

Huge cities that once covered hundreds of square miles are today towns of a hundred acres or so.

Still, driving across lonely prairies, sharp-eyed travelers can yet spot telltale mounds of earth above the wind-whipped grass. If you do, pull over to the side of the road and wait awhile.

Before long, small brown heads with glittering eyes will rise above the dirt and watch you. And when it is determined that you are not a threat, the town will come alive.

Prairie dog mounds average fifty feet apart with grass between. Across the prairie the little animals tussel in play, nurse their young, repair their mounds, visit, quarrel, or just sit and watch the world go by. In short, they do much the same things as any town citizens might do on a sunny afternoon.

If you do get out of the car, do so slowly. And don't slam the door. Otherwise, sharp warning chirps will fill the air, small brown forms will quickly disappear into burrows, and you will find yourself suddenly alone with only the hot prairie wind for company.

THE DEVIL'S ANVIL

Late summer afternoons in Arizona's Sonoran Desert are very still. With spring the desert is glorious with color as wildflowers burst into bloom.

But under summer's merciless and unyeilding sun, the desert becomes what old-time prospectors called the devil's anvil.

Most of the desert animals, hunters and prey alike, lie still in the shade to conserve water. Kit foxes curl up in their dens. Pocket mice and ground squirrels retreat deep into their burrows.

Elf owls doze away the hot hours in nests dug deep into the sheltering arms of saguara cactuses.

With evening the desert creatures begin to stir. As the sun sets, now a dull red ball in the haze, the jagged mountains cast long shadows across the sand. The rocks will be warm to the touch well into evening. But the Sonoran Desert cools rapidly, and there is already a nip in the air.

In the twilight, a roadrunner fights a duel with a rattlesnake. Its rattles buzzing furiously, the snake whips forward, striking at the bird. But the roadrunner nimbly dodges each attack.

Eventually the snake tires and the strikes grow fewer and more sluggish. The roadrunner darts forward, its beak like a fencer's foil. The duel is quickly ended. Under a rising moon, the roadrunner feeds.

In mountain caves, the fetid air stirs as thousands of bats awake and stretch their wings. Hungry, they pour out into the desert night like a sack of pebbles poured out onto the sand.

FLIGHT OF THE PRONGHORN

To watch a band of pronghorn antelope in full flight is to be astonished.

With the first scent of danger on the prairie wind, the great head snaps up and the body tenses. Almost imperceptibly, the large pointed ears sweep the wind for any discernable sound, and dilated black eyes scan the horizon.

On the animal's rump, a signal flag of white hair bristles an alarm, and glands release a special warning scent. Other pronghorns in the band, picking up the scent or seeing the bristling white warning flag, pass on the alarm. With a brisk trot the band closes up into a compact unit.

When the danger is confirmed, perhaps a marauding coyote, an appropriate response is determined. A pronghorn buck in his prime can be an intimidating warrior with horns that draw blood and sharp hooves that kill. But the usual response is swift flight.

As if on command, the entire band bursts forth in a dazzling explosion of speed and agility. If he is not held back by his does and their fawns, a buck can easily hit sixty miles an hour. Bucks have been clocked at forty miles an hour without slowing for several miles. As if guided by a single thought, the band wheels around rolling hills, stopping briefly to check for danger, then abruptly taking off again in flight.

Barbed wire fences and irrigation ditches do not even slow the antelope. With huge soaring leaps, they sail over the obstacles and continue on their way.

Then, as suddenly as it began, the flight ceases. The danger is past but instinct dictates a last sweep of the horizon. Reassured, the antelope nibble at the brown prairie grass.

BIRTH OF THE SPRING FAWNS

When spring comes to Yosemite National Park high in the Sierra Nevada Mountains, the dogwood trees burst into exuberant blossom. Waterfalls flush with snowmelt tumble off rocky crags into the icy Merced River, and the emerald meadows around Mirror Lake are spotted with bright yellow wildflowers.

It is the season when female deer, the does, give birth to their spring fawns. The time of birth is seemingly spontaneous. Some fawns are born in sunlit meadow while others arrive in shadowed groves of trees.

If the doe has not given birth before, there will more than likely be only a single fawn. Otherwise there will usually be twins or even triplets.

Within moments of their birth, the fawns stand uncertainly on thin shivering legs. After a quick cleaning by the doe, the fawns are led away from their birthspot. The doe is most vulnerable while giving birth and she senses that predators may be near.

The doe does not take her fawns far. Most deer live out their lives within a square mile. Soon she selects a spot to place her fawns. Camouflaged by their speckled baby coats, the fawns blend into the forest floor.

When Yosemite's visitors encounter a bear, common sense usually prevails and the animal is left alone. Yet when hikers stumble on a fawn, they frequently cannot resist touching it, stroking its fur, and taking snapshots, all the while unaware of a silent danger.

While the fawn lies motionless, the nearby doe might very well leap to its defense, using her deadly sharp hooves as a weapon. Although she is a frail and delicate-looking creature, the doe can be as deadly as the bear.

148

Photo Opposite
NEWBORN
Len Rue, Jr./H. Armstrong Roberts, Inc.

RACCOONS

Once upon a time, like a zillion other small boys, I lusted for a coonskin cap complete with tail.

On TV I faithfully watched Davy Crockett battle river pirates, run for congress, and go down gloriously at the Alamo. Actually, I was never convinced that he died at the Alamo since he wasn't really shown being killed. All we ever saw was him swinging his rifle "Old Betsy" like a Louisville Slugger, followed by a quick fade to the commercial.

Since then I have been to the Alamo and the folks there (who surely ought to know) say that (1) he certainly was killed and (2) there is no real proof that he actually wore a coonskin cap. So it's just as well that I never got my cap.

Besides, I've come to like the raccoon and he deserves better than to become an adornment for small boys. I'm not alone in my attachment. With his striped tail and burglar masked face, the raccoon is a treat to see in the wild.

And he is, after all, one of our most American animals, being found in every state save Hawaii. His name comes down to us from the Algonquin Indian word *arakun*, which translates roughly as "he who scratches with his hands."

I've read that there's no proof the raccoon actually washes his food before eating, as popularly thought. Some scientists think he's more of a dunker, as in donut dunker. The washing theory has pretty well been consigned to the dustbin.

But I'm still not convinced that Davy Crockett never wore a coonskin cap.

MICHIGAN'S UPPER PENINSULA

If there are ghosts in the deep forests of Michigan's Upper Peninsula, they probably speak French. For a century French frontiersmen trapped in its streams and reveled in its isolation.

The French were pushed aside by the British. But the splendid and wild isolation of the Upper Peninsula continues.

It is both protected by and a captive of water. Lakes Michigan and Huron join forces to separate it from the more populated and sedate south. At the same time, Lake Superior washes against and often lashes its long northern flank.

The Upper Peninsula is a world away from the familiar Michigan of lush farmlands and industrial cities.

It is a place where the crackling of brush signals black bear browsing among the berry bushes. A sudden blur of fur darting through the undergrowth marks a snowshoe hare fleeing a bobcat. Otter and beaver play in the streams, their fur glistening in the ice water.

Just off the coast in the cool, deep waters of Lake Superior is rugged Isle Royale National Park. At first its shoreline appears forbidding, rocky and dense with stands of fir and spruce.

But come up from the beach in this island refuge to where the lakes are surrounded with birch and maple and red oak. Here the world that long ago called the French trappers to the Upper Peninsula has been protected and preserved.

Moose step from the forest shadows. Eagles soar in the sky. And at night the forests of Isle Royale resound to the song of the timber wolf.

Photo Opposite
MOOSE
David Blankenship/New England Stock Photo

SQUIRREL CONNOISSEUR

Being a travel writer has allowed me to become something of a squirrel connoisseur.

I don't mean wilderness squirrels, beautiful though they are. The Kaibab squirrel with its proud white tail is as much a symbol of the Grand Canyon as the blue jays fluttering among the piñons. And you never forget the first sight of a Florida flying squirrel gliding from pine to pine in the Okefenokee twilight.

No, I mean that part pint-sized artist and part hit-and-run burglar, the sassy, brassy city park squirrel.

Take the squirrels of San Diego's Balboa Park. The park, one of the most lovely in the country, is home to theaters, museums, and the world-renowned San Diego Zoo. It is criss-crossed by miles of tree-shaded pathways. And behind every other tree waits a squirrel in ambush.

You're strolling peacefully down the path when suddenly, a squirrel dashes out and blocks your way. With sharp chirping noises, he demands tribute. If it's not forthcoming, he'll allow you to pass. But be prepared to be thoroughly chewed out in Squirrel.

Some Balboa Park squirrels, not content with highway robbery, have broken into the zoo. There they happily compete with the residents for tidbits. But then it's not easy being an inner-city squirrel.

On the other hand, the squirrels in Fresno's Courthouse Park are extremely pleasant. When that central California city built its new courthouse, there were no squirrels in the park. So, several wild squirrels were auditioned and released.

And, knowing how lucky they are, they have impeccable manners.

THE EVERGLADES

Floating silently in a canoe deep in the Florida Everglades, the solitude wraps itself around you and pulls you in. The air is heavy with humidity and the sound of insects. The sea of grass rolls endlessly onward, broken here and there by small islands dotted with trees. But the solitude is an illusion. Every move you make is watched by uncounted glittering eyes.

For all of its primeval beauty, the Florida Everglades are not a place that seems to welcome us. The saw grass, which can grow up to twelve feet, is sharp enough to cut deeply and painfully. Rattlesnakes and water moccasins slither along the water's glassy surface. Alligators laze in the sun and wait for the unwary.

But then, we have not been good to the Everglades. In 1906 Florida began sucking the life water out of the swamps to make way for farms. The land grew tinder dry and the deep wells were poisoned by saltwater seeping in from the ocean.

Fortunately the Everglades have always had fierce defenders. The terrible mistake was realized and restoration began. In 1947 the Everglades National Park was dedicated.

What we finally understood was that the Everglades are a vast nursery teeming with life. Herons, spoonbills, and storks wade through its waters. Eagles perch in the trees. Armadillos poke through the underbrush, and manatees with doleful eyes munch on water hyacinth. There are bear and deer and the occasional scream of a panther across the water.

The Everglades are still under assault. Half have been drained and fires nibble at dried-out areas. And there are people who covet what water remains.

Still there are places left where it is possible to paddle into the dawn and to pause and watch a Great Blue Heron stretch its wings and fly into the rising sun.

Photo Opposite
PANTHER IN COLLIER COUNTY, FL
FLORIDA GAME AND FRESH
WATER COMMISSION
David S. Maehr, Photographer

TRAIL RIDGE ROAD
ROCKY MOUNTAIN NATIONAL PARK COLORADO
Gene Ahrens, Photographer

There are hermit souls that live withdrawn
  In the peace of their self-content;
There are souls like stars that dwell apart,
  In a fellowless firmament;

There are pioneer souls that blaze their paths
  Where highways never ran—
But let me live by the side of the road,
  And be a friend to man.

from "House by the Side of the Road" by Sam Walter Foss

159

ABOUT THE AUTHOR

Michael McKeever has a long-standing love for the backroads of America. In this volume, he has pulled information, feelings, and insights gained from his travels to point out the many places and scenes we so often miss.

McKeever's writing career has led him all over the United States, researching and writing stories. In 1978 he was nominated for an Emmy award for his writing for a local television series, *About San Diego*. He has also written a book about the city entitled *A Short History of San Diego*.

Born in a small fishing village in the Pacific Northwest, McKeever has never lost the small-town touch that shines through in his writing. During his career as a travel writer for magazines like *Country Inns*, McKeever has stayed in resort hotels and luxurious vacation spots all over the United States. Yet his real interest lies in exploring the small towns of America that are so full of life and history.

"The interstate system in this country has made it easy to go from place to place so quickly," says McKeever, "that Americans no longer really look at the land they live in. When I was approached about writing *Backroads of America*, I saw it as a wonderful opportunity to explore the out-of-the-way places we overlook. I never intended for this book to be a literal travel guide. The backroads of our society and our country's history are fascinating, yet they are relatively unknown. So often we just hurry through great historical and cultural landmarks without taking time to stop, look, and listen.

"*Backroads of America* gave me a chance to settle down and write about what I think is important in life. Collecting seashells with my daughter Penny, pulling over at a scenic overlook, and taking the time to really see the land and the people around us—these are important. This is the attitude that I've tried to bring out in *Backroads of America*."